WHICH, BEING INTERPRETED, MEANS . . .

WHICH, BEING INTERPRETED, MEANS . . .

Jack Taylor

 The SeedSowers

Published by
Humor-risk, a division of SeedSowers Publishing House,
PO Box 285, Sargent, GA 30275

ISBN: 0-940232-54-5

CIP: 96-069329

A DISCLAIMER . . .
(OR WHATEVER!)

I know you believe that you understand what you
think I said; but I am not sure you realize that
what you think you heard is not what I meant!

I hereby promise the reader that this book will be at least
as easy to understand as the statement which appears above.
I would, at the same time, exhort the reader not to try to understand all that is written herein. In the event there is such
an attempt, a headache will likely result!

So may I suggest that you do your mind a favor and give
it the day off. Your noggin' could likely use some rest. Have
fun! Be happy!

I hereby grant you an indulgence to . . .

laugh your head off . . .
   get your feelings hurt . . .
      stick your lip out and pout . . .
         add to or take from . . .
            throw a fit . . .
               start an argument with your neighbor . . .
                  send me an anonymous letter (which I
                    likely will not read!) . . .
                  or whatever comes to your mind!

Lighten up! I'm really not being serious. You are free to use these laughables without blame, credit, or threat of suit. The sound of your laughter is all the pay I ask!* They have already been proved in crowds all over the North American continent.

If you have any pain, remember that it is now a medically proven fact that laughter causes the brain to release a morphine-like substance into the blood stream which actually serves to relieve pain.

So put on your old grungy bath robe, relax, and let's walk through fields of laughter! Let's laugh at ourselves.

Your Travel Agent on The Journey of Mirth,
Jack Taylor

---

*Publisher note: We are glad to hear of this decision from Jack; we have no plans to pay him any royalties for this book!

PERSPECTIVE

I love language. It proves handy when it comes to talking (or writing). I am helplessly intrigued with words and their usages. I wish I could speak in every language in use on the planet. But until then I will happily settle for trying to use the one with which I write and speak as aptly as possible.

This book was slowly given birth across the years as I have listened to people of all kinds using our wonderful language. In different times and different places I have witnessed the language seriously handicapped or greatly enhanced by provincial usages. The same words are used differently from area to area, from profession to profession, from era to era. Time does influence the use of words. I remember when gay meant joyous, aids were something that helped you, and Megs were girls named Margaret. Now gay means different, and aids kill you, and whatever megs are my computer has 40 of them.

I am a Christian and a public speaker as well as an author. I move among varying religious groups in a widening (and gladdening) circle. I listen to strange usages of the language all the time. Just as attorneys speak "legalese" and the medical world uses "doctorspeak," Christians are given to speaking varying forms of "Christianese." I doubt that the world around us knows what we are saying when we speak. I'll go a step farther and say that I doubt that we know what each other is saying much of the time. In fact, I often wonder if we know what we are saying ourselves.

I was born again into the Christian faith when I was a child. I began to pick up labels and terms way back then. I have been doing so ever since. It would help me if every few years we could have a clarification of terms. This would likely serve to clarify many of the mysteries in our language processes. It is toward this goal of clarification that I point the purpose of this little volume, a sort of glossary of terms for Christians. A quick-reference handbook to decipher "Christianese."

Acronyms, euphemisms, initialisms and metaphors dot the landscape of literature and public speaking. I was recently in the hospital for an extended time. The whole medical system is a world of strange languages. I learned the meaning of some terms and was sorry that I had at times.

What you are about to read is a tongue-in-cheek endeavor to promote mutual understanding among Christians, an encouragement for us to mean what we say and say what we mean. I have entitled it *Which, Being Interpreted, Means,* because much of the time what we are really saying is not what we mean. When we come to that section you will notice that the first statement will be entitled "TIWYH" (for This is what you heard . . .) and the second, "WBIM" (for Which, Being Interpreted, Means . . .)

The too-serious-minded reader will often need to be reminded that this is tongue-in-cheek stuff and not doctrinal material. "Lighten up!," will be the appropriate advice as you open this tome to read it. So read it in the spirit in which I write it—gratefully, joyously, and laughingly.

HERE'S TO LAUGHTER!

Laughter originated with God and is among the greatest gifts from God to mankind. "He that sits in the heavens shall laugh," declared the Psalmist in Psalm 2:4.

Laughter is a remarkable phenomenon whether it is approached from the medical, psychological or sociological standpoint. Recent research in the field of laughter is revealing astounding implications in the physiological as well as the psychological realms. In addition to this the effects of laughter in the sociological and spiritual are almost limitless.

I recently walked into a meeting of folks who had just discovered that an investment plan had bellied up and they had lost everything they had put into it. I was one of them! Everyone in the room had worried looks. One was crying and others were ashen grey with shock. Two in the room had lost everything they had including their jobs. Our lawyer would soon arrive and help us to study our recourses.

The situation was somber indeed. I was suddenly seized with a spirit of frivolity. I said, "I feel like the Calvinist who fell down the stairs; he got up, dusted himself off, and said with delight, 'Man, I'm glad to have that behind me!'" Other silly statements followed. The next thing we knew everyone was laughing. One sitting next to me said, "Folks coming into this meeting are going to think they are in the wrong group!" Our laughter brought relief and prepared us to discuss the serious developments with clear heads.

Laughter is a safety valve in the human psyche which often prevents a destructive emotional explosion.

It is a declaration of unshaken confidence without words.

It dulls the keen edge of anger and is a soothing balm on many other destructive emotions.

It reconnects frayed nerves and allows regaining of proper perspective.

It delivers us from the continuing peril of taking ourselves too seriously.

It may yield more calm than a tranquilizer, more energy than a vitamin, more excitement than a shot of adrenaline.

Laughter can turn a potential battlefield into a picnic; a church fight into a lovefest.

It is virtually impossible to laugh too much; it is likely that we all laugh too little.

Every situation has a "laugh zone" and we had best learn to repair away to it frequently.

Every area of our existence is mined with rich veins of material for the laughter mill . . . marriage, childbirth, school, politics, and yes, even pain and sickness.

But no area of our lives is so packed with "laughables" as our church life where Christians walk, talk, and think (sometimes).

I have divided the materials in *Which, Being Interpreted, Means* . . . into divisions suitable for reference such as what preachers say to people, what people say to preachers and what Christians say to one another. Read and laugh!

It would be well for the Christian world to do what President Harry S. Truman threatened to do in a mock memorandum during his time in the White House:

> I have appointed a Secretary of Semantics, a most important post. He is to furnish me with forty and fifty-dollar words that tell me how to say no and yes in the same sentence without contradiction. He is to tell me the combination of words that will put me

against inflation in San Francisco and for it in New York. He is to show me how to be silent and say everything. You can see how he can save me an immense amount of worry.

I want to be the first to apply for this post in the Christian world.

Jack Taylor, Applicant: SECRETARY OF SEMANTICS
(Watch the initialism on that one!)

WHICH, BEING
INTERPRETED,
MEANS . . .

This is what you heard . . .

"I'll pray about it."

Which, being interpreted, means . . .

This is what you heard . . .

"I have a check in
my spirit."

Which, being interpreted, means . . .

This is what you heard . . .

"My spirit bears
witness to that."

Which, being interpreted, means . . .

"I'm not going to say,
'I told you so.'"

"I'm laughing with
you, not at you."

"BOY HOWDY, ARE YOU EVER A JOKE!"

"I really do love you."

"MORE THAN CHESS, AS MUCH
AS BASEBALL, AND ALMOST AS
MUCH AS FOOTBALL!"

"I'm not really forgetful."

"FOR GOODNESS SAKE, I REMEMBERED OUR ANNIVERSARY EIGHT YEARS AGO!"

"Son, just read what
the Bible says about
sex."

"HOW MANY TIMES DO
I HAVE TO TELL YOU,
I KNOW NOTHING ABOUT
THE SUBJECT!"

"Now, don't
misunderstand me."

"Now, I don't mean to be critical."

"YOU AND I BOTH KNOW THAT I'M ABOUT TO BE AS CRITICAL AS THE DEVIL!"

"Brother, you know
I'm open to that."

"I PLUMB DON'T BELIEVE IT YET!"

"Brethren, we need to move slowly on this issue."

"HECK NO — WE WON'T GO!"

"Brother, just trust the Lord."

"I have the gift of prophecy."

"GIVE ME A BREAK —I HAVE TO HAVE SOME WAY TO JUSTIFY HOW MEAN I AM!"

"I have a word from God for you."

"I'M ABOUT TO BLAST YOU,
BUT BLAMING GOD MAY KEEP
YOU FROM TAKING REVENGE!"

"This is a faith ministry."

WBIM

"The Lord just gave us a new car!"

"WE WANTED A NEW CAR LIKE THE JONESES AND HOCKED OURSELVES UP TO OUR EARS IN DEBT, HOPING THAT GOD WILL HONOR OUR GREED AND PRESUMPTION."

"Now, I'm a'fixin' to tell you the unvarnished truth."

"I'M ABOUT TO LIE IN YOUR FACE ALL OVER THE PLACE!"

"Oh, I'm hanging in there."

"HELP! I'VE FALLEN DOWN
AND I CAN'T GET BACK UP!"

"Don't worry about your illness, brother, just believe."

"GIVE ME TIME TO GET OUT OF HERE SO I WON'T BE AROUND WHEN YOU FIND OUT NOTHING HAS HAPPENED!"

"Now, I don't mean to gossip."

"I HAVE A JUICY BIT OF
GOSSIP I JUST CAN'T
WAIT TO UNLOAD!"

"We have just taken our greatest step of faith."

"I THINK WE'RE IN BIIIIIIG TROUBLE!"

"God is really purging our fellowship."

"I'M FAILING, THE SHIP'S SINKING, THE RATS ARE JUMPING OVERBOARD — AND I WOULD TOO IF I HAD SOMEWHERE TO GO!"

"Pastor, I've been behind you all these years."

"I'd like a minute
of your time if
you don't mind."

"I PLAN TO HOG YOUR TIME FOR ABOUT AN HOUR!"

"Pastor, your sermons are like manna to me."

WBIM

"YOUR SERMONS SEEM TO COME FROM OUT OF NOWHERE, ARE DULL, DRY, AND TASTELESS! I'M SICK AND TIRED OF THEM AND THEY ROT AFTER TWENTY·FOUR HOURS!"

TIWYH

"Finally, brethren . . ."

"CONSIDER YOURSELF BLESSED
INDEED IF YOU ARE OUT OF
HERE IN LESS THAN AN HOUR!"

"Our worship center was comfortably filled."

"I just don't understand the spiritual gifts."

"I HATE 'EM!"

"Sorry, pastor,
that's just not in
my area of gifting."

"I JUST FLAT OUT DON'T WANT TO DO IT!"

"We had a great church revival."

"NOT ONE CONSARNED, CONTINENTAL THING HAPPENED!"

"After considerable prayer and research . . .

"I'VE PRAYED ABOUT IT ONCE AND THOUGHT ABOUT IT TWICE."

"God has not
released me to work
in the nursery."

"TAKE CARE OF YOUR OWN DIRTY BABY, SALLY — I'VE ALREADY RAISED MINE!"

"This is an original sermon."

"I ONLY STOLE MATERIAL FROM TWO OTHER PREACHERS."

"I just don't feel moved in that direction."

"I DON'T WANT TO DO IT
AND NEEDED A GOOD
SPIRITUAL-SOUNDING EXCUSE!"

"Pastor, I'll be with you in spirit on Sunday morning!"

"SO LONG, PASTOR—
I'M GONE FISHING!"

"Pastor, your
sermon was
warm and moving."

"YOU WERE BLOWING A LOT OF HOT AIR AND I WAS MOVED TO TAKE A NAP!"

"Pastor, everybody's talking about it."

"I HEARD ONE PERSON TALKING ABOUT IT AND ANOTHER SLIGHTLY REFER TO IT."

"Hey, gang, let's go out and have some good Christian fellowship!"

"LET'S GO PIG-OUT AND CALL IT CHRISTIAN FELLOWSHIP!"

This is what you heard . . .

"Lord, I sure do need to hear from you now."

"LORD, I WASN'T ALL THAT IMPRESSED WITH THE LAST THING YOU SAID TO ME."

"You know what
the Bible says,
'Let all things
be done decently
and in order.'"

"I'M SURE GLAD THE BIBLE AGREES WITH ME — I DON'T WANT THAT WEIRD STUFF GOING ON IN MY CHURCH."

"I could go on and on . . ."

"IN FACT, THAT'S WHAT I'M GONNA DO — GO ON AND ON AND ON!"

"Bro. So and so is one of God's choicest servants."

"I CAN'T THINK OF ONE GOOD THING TO SAY ABOUT HIM AND I'LL BE FOREVER GRATEFUL FOR SOMEBODY COMING UP WITH THAT PRETTY CATCH-ALL PHRASE!"

"Man, it was wonderful how my heart was bonded to that brother!"

"We sure do appreciate our former pastor."

"WE'LL SAY THE SAME THING ABOUT YOU AS SOON AS WE CAN MAKE YOU OUR FORMER PASTOR!"

"And don't worry about the honorarium; my church always gives good love-offerings."

"WE GUARANTEE EVERY PREACHER WHO COMES AT LEAST 75 CENTS A SERMON! OF COURSE, WE EXPECT HIM TO PAY HIS OWN TRAVEL EXPENSE!"

"Oh, pastor, we'll pay you what you're worth."

"YOU LOOK LIKE A REAL BARGAIN AND WE WERE LOOKING FOR A DISCOUNT."

"We sure do like our new pastor and he sure is fitting in."

"SO FAR, HE'S DONE EVERYTHING WE'VE TOLD HIM TO DO. IT LOOKS LIKE WE'RE GOING TO BE ABLE TO CONTROL HIM, TOO!"

"Our pastor is so handsome and to think, he's single also!"

"HE'S TOLERABLE TO LOOK
AT SO I THINK I'LL PRAY
MY UGLY OLD·MAID DAUGHTER
ON HIM."

"Our church is going like a house afire."

"OUR CHURCH IS COMPLETELY OUT OF CONTROL, BONKERS, BANANAS, BOING! BOING! BOING!"

"Well, our church is not doing very well right now."

"BUT PRAISE THE LORD, NONE OF THE OTHERS AROUND ARE DOING ANY GOOD EITHER!"

"Pastor, your sermon was like a cup of cold water."

"IN MY FACE, WAKING ME UP ON A COLD MORNING!"

"Pastor, your sermon this morning was like a cool breeze."

WBIM

"COLD AND WINDY!"

"Pastor, your
sermon was deep
and profound."

"YOUR SERMON WAS THE PITS AND I DIDN'T UNDERSTAND A THING YOU SAID."

"I'm beginning
to feel really
good for a change."

"FIRST DAY THIS MONTH
I DON'T FEEL LIKE SHOOTIN'
MYSELF!"

"May I offer you a constructive word of criticism?"

" I SURE HOPE YOU SAY 'YES!' BECAUSE I AM ABOUT TO GET PERMISSION TO STAB YOU STRAIGHT THROUGH THE HEART!"

"Pastor, your sermon certainly made me appreciate the wonders of God's great outdoors."

"PASTOR, WHILE LISTENING TO YOU THIS MORNING I'D RATHER'VE BEEN OUT FISHING OR GOLFING OR ANYWHERE BUT HERE!"

"What showers of
blessings your
sermon brought!"

"I WAS ON THE SECOND ROW AND YOU SPIT ALL OVER ME!"

"Your sermon
certainly was
TIME-ly."

"IT TOOK TOO MUCH AND WOULD HAVE BEEN BETTER AT SOME OTHER!"

"That was a powerful musical presentation!"

"BROKE MY GLASSES
AND BOTH EAR DRUMS!"

"Terrible! Just terrible! But cheer up! It could have been worse."

"IT COULD HAVE HAPPENED TO ME!"

"The Pastor Search Committee has voted for you to be our INTERIM pastor!"

"We just think we'll keep you as our pastor for another fifty years."

WBIM

"TRUTH IS, WE NEVER DID
WANT MUCH OF A PASTOR AND
YOU'RE ABOUT AS NEAR NOTHING
AS WE EVER HAD, SO WE JUST
THOUGHT WE'D KEEP YOU!"

"They're from another persuasion."

"FROM OFF THE PLANET, WEIRDOES, NOT MUCH LIKE US, AND WE WOULDN'T BE CAUGHT DEAD WITH THEM."

"I'd like to announce that I'm giving my offerings to my favorite charities."

"MY WIFE, MY CHILDREN
AND... MY GRANDCHILDREN!"

"We plan to raise our pastor's salary as the church grows."

"WE FIGGER WE'RE PRETTY SAFE SINCE THE CHURCH HAS NOT GROWN FOR FIFTY YEARS AND DOESN'T LOOK TO FOR FIFTY MORE!"

"I believe this is
what God told me."

"THIS SOUNDS SO OFF-THE-WALL THAT I'LL PLAY IT SAFE AND BLAME IT ON GOD."

"I have this strange feeling down deep in my spirit."

"MEAT LOAF FOR SUPPER
AND MY NERVOUS STOMACH
IS THROWING FITS."

"In our church we believe ALL the Bible."

"UNTIL IT CROSSES OUR TRADITION
AND LIFESTYLE — AND THEN, TO
COVER OUR BEHINDS, WE ENGAGE
IN INTERPRETIVE EXPOSITION."

"We're looking for a new pastor and you might be just the man."

"WE'RE LOOKING FOR NOAH'S EXPERIENCE, DAVID'S GIANT-KILLING YOUTHFUL ENTHUSIASM, SAMSON'S DURABILITY AND PAUL'S WILLINGNESS TO WORK WITHOUT REMUNERATION."

"Pastor, I'm afraid that everybody in the church is mad at you."

"MY WIFE AND I HAVE A SERIOUS GRIPE WITH YOU AND ARE CERTAIN THAT ALL THE WISE PEOPLE OF THE CHURCH JOIN US IN OUR COMPLAINT."

"I've come to you representing the *SPIRITUAL* element of the church!"

"You know, I believe we had one of our better business meetings last night."

"I ONLY COUNTED FOURTEEN CUSS WORDS, FOUR SERIOUS ELBOW WOUNDS, SIX MURDEROUS LOOKS AMONG THE DEACONS — AND MY WIFE DIDN'T ONCE BURST INTO TEARS AFTERWARDS!"

"Pastor, we sure do hate to see you go."

"Pastor, your sermons are so feeding to us."

"I'VE HAD ABOUT A BELLY-FULL OF YOUR PREACHING!"

"Our church has just gone through an administrative realignment."

"AH GOT FARRRRRED — AS IN C-A-N-N-E-D, TERMINATED, PINK-SLIPPED, TOLD NOT TO COME BACK... TO VACATE THE PARSONAGE IMMEDIATELY!"

"I really don't expect anything out of this for myself."

"EXCEPT HALF THE PROFITS, ALL THE CREDIT AND 25% OF THE INTERNATIONAL ROYALTIES!"

"Well, I will admit that I've put on a little weight this year."

"I LOOK LIKE A BEAN-BAG WITH ARMS AND LEGS!"

"Being an effective evangelist, my schedule is full and I am in great demand."

"CHRISTMAS, I GO SEE MOM; I HAVE A FEW WEEKS OPEN; AND THE LAST THREE CHURCHES DEMANDED I LEAVE!"

"Just to show you how important I am, I have a special agreement with all the major airlines."

"IF I'M NOT THERE WHEN
THEY GET READY TO LEAVE,
THEY HAVE MY PERMISSION TO
GO ON WITHOUT ME!"

"Lord, I'll go anywhere in this wide world."

"AS LONG AS IT'S NEAR MY FAMILY, HAS HOT AND COLD RUNNING WATER, IS WITHIN WALKING DISTANCE OF A MAJOR MALL AND BLAH, BLAH, BLAH!"

"The time has come for me to get on my face before the Lord."

"I'M ON THE VERGE OF A SERIOUS TWO·HOUR NAP!"

"We came all the way from Detroit to hear you preach."

"ACTUALLY WE CAME TO SEE OUR GRANDKIDS AND YOU JUST HAPPENED TO BE HERE!"

"I think he may have a slight rejection problem."

❧

"HE WAS SO UGLY THE STORK CIRCLED THE HOUSE THREE DAYS BEFORE HE HAD NERVE ENOUGH TO DROP HIM OFF!"

"You are certainly looking healthy and robust."

"WHEN OUR PIGS GOT AS FAT
AS YOU, WE SKINNED 'EM!"

"Remember, Jesus said, 'It is more blessed to give than to receive.'"

"JUST TO SHOW HOW SPIRITUAL I AM, I WILL ALLOW YOU TO HAVE THE GREATER BLESSING OF GIVING WHILE I SIT BACK AND HUMBLY RECEIVE."

"If I've ever seen a heretic, he's one!"

"HE DOESN'T AGREE WITH MY STAND ON INFANT BAPTISM, ETERNAL SECURITY, PREDESTINATION, OR SUNDAY AFTERNOON FOOTBALL."

"I am a member of the church in good standing."

"I'M GOOD AT STANDING AGAINST EVERYTHING OUR PASTOR SUGGESTS!"

"I'm afraid our pastor may be getting too liberal."

"LAST SUNDAY, WHEN HE FINISHED PREACHING, HE WAS WALKING ON SIX INCHES OF HIS TROUSERS LEG, HAD PERSPIRED 3 QUARTS, HAD LOST SIX POUNDS BUT HE COULD SPEAK ABOVE A WHISPER BY TUESDAY!"

"Now, I don't mean to hurt your feelings."

"I'M A FIXIN' TO HURT YOUR FEELINGS BIIIIIIG TIME!"

"Pastor, each one of your sermons is like the grace of God."

"DOESN'T INVOLVE WORKS, IS
NEVER·ENDING AND TOTALLY
IMPOSSIBLE TO UNDERSTAND!"

"We sure did enjoy ourselves."

"WE DIDN'T ENJOY YOU, BUT
WE DID ENJOY OURSELVES."

"Since I retired it seems like I have twice as much to do."

"I GET HALF AS MUCH DONE AND IT TAKES TWICE AS LONG."

"I don't seem to have quite as much energy as I used to have."

"WHEN I SIT IN A ROCKING CHAIR, I HAVE A HARD TIME GETTING IT GOING!"

"As I get older I do have a few more aches and pains."

"EVERYTHING HURTS — AND WHAT DON'T HURT DON'T WORK!"

"In light of recent events we are thinking of renaming our church."

"Dr. Calm N. Peece seems to be so laid back and relaxed."

"HIS SEMINARY GRADUATION PRESENT WAS A FRONTAL LOBOTOMY!"

"My spiritual gift is exhortation."

"AN EXCELLENT COVERUP
FOR COWARDICE AND
COMPROMISE!"

"Now that I'm getting older, I get confused at times."

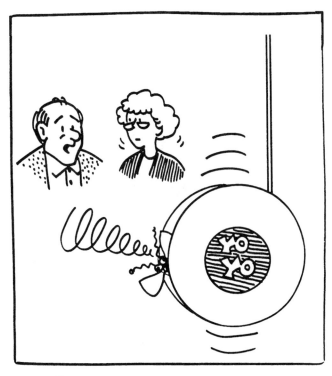

"HALF THE TIME I FEEL AS DISORIENTED AS A TERMITE IN A YO-YO!"

"Our Christmas Pageant went off much better this year than last."

WBIM

"LAST YEAR BRO. SOURNOTE FELL INTO THE ORCHESTRA PIT, THE CAMEL BURPED ON THE CLARINET PLAYER, THE LIVING CHRISTMAS TREE PANCAKED DOWN TO TWO LEVELS, AND THE DONKEY DROP-KICKED SISTER LOUDLUNG INTO THE BAPTISTRY!"

"I heard the Lord call me into evangelism."

"THE LAST THREE YEARS OF STATISTICS IN OUR CHURCH REALLY IMPROVED MY HEARING!"

"I trust God will speak to you today."

"HE'D BETTER BECAUSE I
DON'T HAVE THE SLIGHTEST
IDEA WHAT TO TELL YOU!"

Books by Jack Taylor

The Key to Triumphant Living
The Hallelujah Factor
God's Plan of Economy
The Word of God with Power
Which, Being Interpreted, Means . . . .

Other Books by Jack Taylor
Available in Limited Supply

Much More
After the Spirit Comes
Prayer: Life's Limitless Reach
Victory Over the Devil
One Home Under God
God's New Creation

by Barbara Taylor

From Rejection to Acceptance

ABOUT THE AUTHOR

Jack Taylor . . .

is a native of Texas living in Florida. He is founder and president of Dimensions Ministries, a pastor for more than 25 years and former vice-president of the Southern Baptist Convention. His present ministry takes him around the world among varying Christian groups with a continuing emphasis on both personal and corporate revival.

He has spoken across North America and around the world in Africa, Russia, Europe, Asia, Israel, Taiwan, the Philippines, Singapore and Indonesia. He has authored eleven books across twenty-five years including *The Key to Triumphant Living, Much More, One Home Under God, After the Spirit Comes, What Every Husband Should Know, God's New Creation, God's Miraculous Plan of Economy, Prayer: Life's Limitless Reach, Victory Over the Devil, The Hallelujah Factor,* and his latest, *The World of God With Power.* His wife, Barbara, has one best seller to her credit, *From Rejection to Acceptance.*

Though Jack frequently utilizes humor in preaching this is his first journalistic venture into satire and "tongue in cheek" fun with Christian conversation.

JOE M. McKEEVER—ARTIST

Joe and his wife Margaret make their home in Kenner, LA where he is pastor of the First Baptist Church. He is a graduate of Birmington-Southern College and holds Th.M. and D.Min. degrees from New Orleans Baptist Theological Seminary.